T0198889

Are You In The Meow?

Allowing Your Cat to Guide You to Enlightenment

by **Neko**

Translation and Illustrations by

Karen LeCocq

All we ever have is now. Meow.

To order additional copies of this book, contact:
Xlibris
844-714-8691
www.Xlibris.com
Orders@Xlibris.com

| ISBN: | Softcover | 978-1-4134-7147-2 |
| | Hardcover | 978-1-4134-7164-9 |

Library of Congress Control Number: 2004097769

Print information available on the last page

Rev. date: 05/04/2023

Cats know nothing of Zen. We just live it.

Human

Cats watch humans. We see that some live in the present time, but others appear tense and in some other place as they hurry through their days.

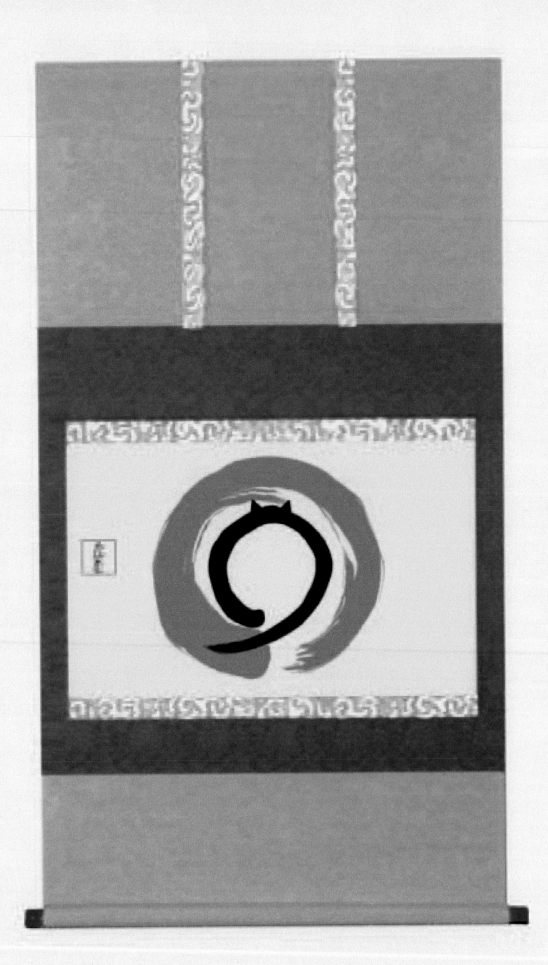

Some inquiring humans have pondered the question, "What is it that makes my cat so centered, calm, and at peace with the world?"

Right Now

It is all very simple. Cats just do what they do; and they do it with an alert presence. We walk. We eat. We wash ourselves. We run. We sit down. We play and we sleep. We pay attention to what we do. Our whole cat being is right here, now, in whatever we are doing.

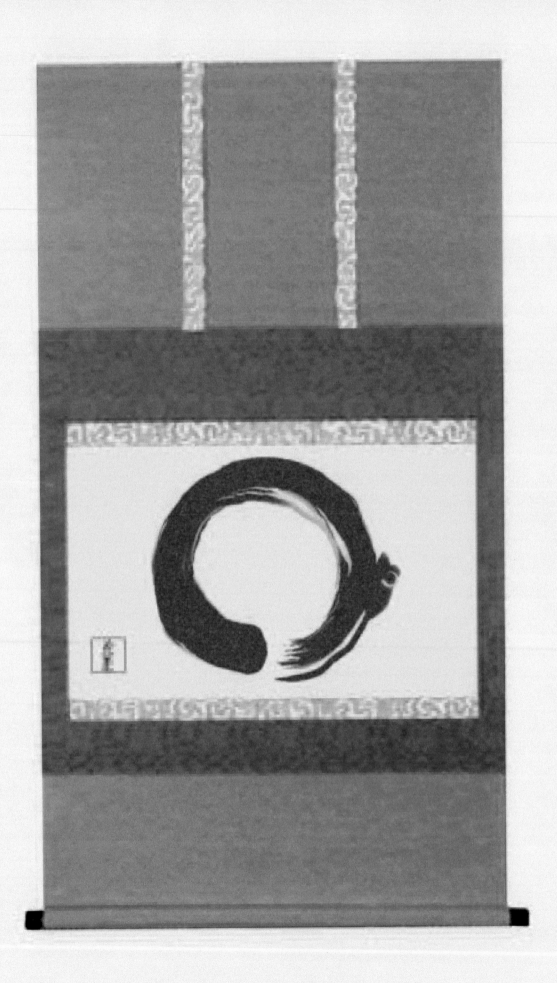

When we play, we just simply play. There is no
need to understand what play is. There is no need
to think about playing. We just play.

Cats aren't aware of the past, only what is happening right now in the present. We watch the world around us and see each thing as if we have never seen it before. All things are new.

Truth

Cats pay attention to what they do. When eating, we focus on the food in the bowl, nothing else.

Cats notice every detail of their surroundings.
When a new catnip plant springs up, we are right
on top of it.

Peaceful

When we sit, we do it with a watchful consciousness, always in the present.

Tranquility

And when we nap, we really nap all the way.
You might say, we become the nap.

24

When we wake, we are fully alert and alive.

When you pay attention and notice everything, you are in the now. At times, humans seem to be somewhere other than right here. As cat, we do what we can to lead our human friends into the present time.

Awake

We jump up in human laps when they least expect it. That brings them into the moment.

Life Energy

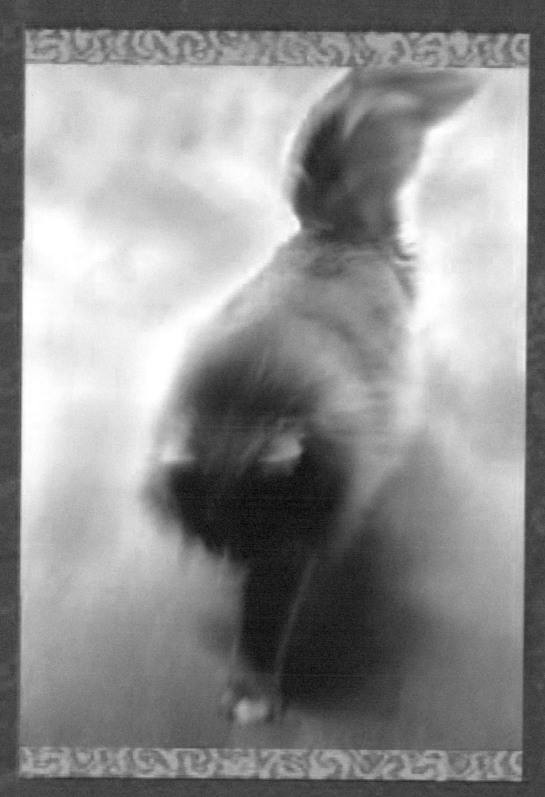

We run through the house at night going so quickly one can barely see us. Our humans look up and take notice.

Be Encouraged

Sometimes we claw or bite, but only as a last resort. It is an effective way to bring one into the present time.

Offer

Perhaps the most effective method to bring a human into the present time is to utter one single "Meow." It has such a beautiful ring against the silence. Repetitive meows tend to get on human nerves, but a single, well placed meow is like a bell. It gently brings one into the now.

Friend

In their own charming way, cats are doing their humans a favor. We are allowing you to be right here, right now, enjoying the present with your feline friend.

Wisdom

It is no coincidence that Meow and Now are so similar in sound. Cats throughout the ages have been dwelling in the present moment we call "The Meow".

As a wise human once said, "You are Buddha,
and you are ordinary cat mind." *

Clarity

sitting quietly, doing nothing, spring comes, and
the catnip grows by itself. **

Listen

If you listen carefully, you will hear when your cat is leading you into "The Meow". Follow please. Receive our special gift to our human friends.

Neko

Sachi

Tommy

猫

Neko
cat

About the Author:

Neko lives very much in the present time in a loft/ studio space in Merced, California. He shares his space with two humans and two fellow cats, Sachi and Tommy, who are featured in this book. Neko can be reached through his web site: www.nekocat.net.

Kalin
water lilly

About the Translator and Illustrator:

Karen LeCocq lives and works in the same space as Neko, Sachi, Tommy and her husband, David Medley. Both Karen and David write and make art. Karen's children's book, **Neko In New York**, is available at Neko's web site or at Karen's site: www.karenlecocq.com, where you can also view some of her sculpture. Her Japanese teacher gave her the name Kalin.

Paw notes:

* The actual quote from Shunryu Suzuki was, "You are Buddha, and you are ordinary mind".
** The real Zen Proverb is "Sitting quietly, doing nothing, spring comes, and the grass grows by itself."
The fly illustration was adapted from Shunryu Suzuki's book, **Zen Mind, Beginner's Mind**.

Printed in the United States
by Baker & Taylor Publisher Services